EMMANUEL JOSEPH

The Innovator's Heart, Emotional Intelligence, Cultural Insight, and Ethical Entrepreneurship

Copyright © 2025 by Emmanuel Joseph

All rights reserved. No part of this publication may be reproduced, stored or transmitted in any form or by any means, electronic, mechanical, photocopying, recording, scanning, or otherwise without written permission from the publisher. It is illegal to copy this book, post it to a website, or distribute it by any other means without permission.

First edition

This book was professionally typeset on Reedsy. Find out more at reedsy.com

Contents

1	Chapter 1: The Soul of Innovation	1
2	Chapter 2: Embracing Diversity	3
3	Chapter 3: Ethical Foundations	5
4	Chapter 4: Building Emotional Resilience	7
5	Chapter 5: Understanding Cultural Nuances	9
6	Chapter 5: Understanding Cultural Nuances	11
7	Chapter 6: Ethical Decision-Making	13
8	Chapter 7: Emotional Intelligence in Leadership	15
9	Chapter 8: Cultural Adaptability	17
10	Chapter 8: Cultural Adaptability	19
11	Chapter 9: Ethical Entrepreneurship in Practice	21
12	Chapter 10: Emotional Intelligence in Collaboration	23
13	Chapter 11: Cultural Insight in Market Research	25
14	Chapter 12: Ethical Marketing	27
15	Chapter 13: Emotional Intelligence in Negotiation	29
16	Chapter 14: Cultural Sensitivity in Product Development	31
17	Chapter 15: Ethical Supply Chain Management	33
18	Chapter 16: Emotional Intelligence in Customer Relations	36
19	Chapter 17: The Future of Ethical Innovation	38

1

Chapter 1: The Soul of Innovation

Innovation isn't just about creating new products or services—it's about fostering a culture that values emotional intelligence. Emotional intelligence, or EI, refers to the ability to recognize, understand, and manage our own emotions, while also empathizing with the emotions of others. At the heart of innovation lies the human touch. Innovators who harness EI are able to build strong, cohesive teams, navigate challenges with resilience, and create solutions that resonate on a deeper level with their audience. They understand that innovation is not just a process but a mindset. **Emotional intelligence is a cornerstone of true innovation**, enabling leaders to connect with their teams and customers on a profound level, driving both creativity and collaboration.

In the fast-paced world of entrepreneurship, the ability to remain emotionally balanced can make or break an endeavor. Innovators who maintain emotional equilibrium can steer their ventures through turbulent times, inspiring confidence and trust in their stakeholders. Emotional intelligence allows leaders to navigate the complexities of human relationships, fostering an environment where diverse ideas can flourish. **Innovation thrives where empathy and understanding prevail**—it's about more than just the end product; it's about the journey and the connections made along the way.

The innovators who excel are those who see beyond the immediate and the tangible. They recognize the importance of nurturing the emotional well-being of their teams, understanding that a motivated, engaged workforce is essential to sustained success. Emotional intelligence is not a static trait but a skill that can be developed and honed over time. By investing in their own emotional growth and encouraging the same in others, innovators can create a ripple effect that transforms their organizations and the wider community.

Ultimately, the soul of innovation lies in its ability to touch hearts and minds. By embracing emotional intelligence, innovators can create a legacy that goes beyond profits and products, making a lasting impact on the world. They can cultivate a culture where creativity and compassion coexist, driving forward not just technological advancements but also meaningful social change. **This is the true essence of innovation—changing the world, one empathetic interaction at a time.**

2

Chapter 2: Embracing Diversity

True innovation thrives in an environment rich in cultural diversity. When different perspectives converge, they create a fertile ground for groundbreaking ideas. Embracing cultural insight means recognizing the value that each individual's background and experiences bring to the table. It's about fostering an inclusive environment where diverse voices are not just heard, but valued and respected. By doing so, innovators can uncover hidden opportunities and develop solutions that are truly representative of the global market.

Diversity fuels creativity. When teams are composed of individuals with varied experiences and worldviews, they are more likely to approach problems from unique angles and devise innovative solutions. **Embracing diversity requires more than just token representation—it involves creating a culture where all team members feel empowered to contribute**. Innovators must actively seek out and celebrate different perspectives, ensuring that their organizations are as inclusive as they are dynamic.

In a globalized world, understanding cultural nuances is essential for innovators. By appreciating and respecting cultural differences, they can build stronger relationships with international partners, tailor their solutions to meet local needs, and avoid potential misunderstandings. Cultural insight goes hand-in-hand with emotional intelligence, enabling innovators to navigate the complexities of human interactions with grace and sensitivity.

This holistic approach to innovation ensures that solutions are not only effective but also culturally relevant.

Diversity also extends beyond cultural and ethnic backgrounds—it encompasses a range of experiences, skills, and perspectives. Innovators should strive to create multidisciplinary teams that bring together experts from different fields. This cross-pollination of ideas can lead to unexpected breakthroughs, as team members draw on their unique expertise to tackle challenges in new and creative ways. **By fostering a culture of collaboration and respect, innovators can harness the full potential of diversity to drive their ventures forward.**

Ultimately, embracing diversity is about recognizing the inherent value of every individual and creating an environment where everyone can thrive. Innovators who prioritize diversity and inclusion are better positioned to create solutions that resonate with a broad audience, ensuring that their impact is both far-reaching and profound. **By championing diversity, innovators can create a more equitable and innovative world, where every voice is heard and every idea has the potential to make a difference.**

3

Chapter 3: Ethical Foundations

Ethical entrepreneurship is the cornerstone of sustainable innovation. Innovators must be guided by a strong sense of integrity, ensuring that their actions align with their values. This involves not only adhering to legal standards but also considering the broader impact of their innovations on society and the environment. Ethical entrepreneurs are transparent in their dealings, prioritize long-term value over short-term gains, and are committed to making a positive difference in the world.

Ethics in entrepreneurship goes beyond compliance with laws and regulations—it encompasses a commitment to doing what is right, even when it is difficult. Innovators must be willing to make tough decisions that align with their principles, even if it means sacrificing short-term profits. **Ethical entrepreneurship requires a deep understanding of the impact of one's actions on all stakeholders, including employees, customers, communities, and the environment.**

Transparency is a key component of ethical entrepreneurship. Innovators must be open and honest in their communications, building trust with their stakeholders through consistent and clear messaging. This transparency extends to all aspects of the business, from financial reporting to marketing practices. By being transparent, ethical entrepreneurs can create a culture of trust and accountability, fostering stronger relationships with their stakeholders.

Ethical entrepreneurship also involves a commitment to sustainability. Innovators must consider the long-term impact of their actions on the environment and society, striving to create solutions that are both innovative and sustainable. This includes reducing waste, conserving resources, and supporting initiatives that promote social and environmental well-being. **By prioritizing sustainability, ethical entrepreneurs can create lasting value for their stakeholders and contribute to a better future for all**.

In essence, ethical entrepreneurship is about aligning one's actions with one's values and making decisions that prioritize the greater good. Innovators who embrace ethical principles are better positioned to create solutions that are not only effective but also responsible and sustainable. **By leading with integrity and a commitment to ethical principles, innovators can build a legacy that extends beyond their individual ventures, inspiring others to follow in their footsteps and create a positive impact on the world.**

4

Chapter 4: Building Emotional Resilience

Emotional resilience is the ability to adapt to stress and adversity without compromising one's well-being. For innovators, this quality is crucial, as the path to innovation is often fraught with obstacles. Building emotional resilience involves developing coping strategies, maintaining a positive outlook, and seeking support when needed. Innovators who possess emotional resilience are better equipped to navigate setbacks, learn from failures, and continue pushing forward with determination and creativity.

Resilience is not about avoiding challenges but about facing them head-on and finding ways to overcome them. Innovators must develop a growth mindset, viewing setbacks as opportunities for learning and growth rather than as insurmountable obstacles. **By cultivating a positive and proactive attitude, innovators can maintain their focus and drive, even in the face of adversity**.

One of the key aspects of building emotional resilience is developing effective coping strategies. This can include practices such as mindfulness, meditation, and exercise, which help to reduce stress and promote emotional well-being. Innovators should also prioritize self-care, ensuring that they take the time to rest and recharge, so they can approach their work with renewed energy and enthusiasm.

Support networks are also essential for building emotional resilience.

Innovators should seek out mentors, peers, and other sources of support who can provide guidance, encouragement, and perspective. **By surrounding themselves with a strong support network, innovators can draw on the collective wisdom and experience of others, helping them to navigate challenges with greater confidence and resilience**.

Ultimately, emotional resilience is about maintaining a sense of balance and perspective, even in the face of adversity. Innovators who possess emotional resilience are better equipped to navigate the ups and downs of the entrepreneurial journey, maintaining their focus and drive in the face of challenges. **By cultivating emotional resilience, innovators can not only achieve their goals but also enjoy a greater sense of well-being and fulfillment along the way**.

5

Chapter 5: Understanding Cultural Nuances

In a globalized world, understanding cultural nuances is essential for innovators. Cultural insight involves recognizing the subtle differences in communication styles, values, and social norms across different cultures. Innovators who take the time to understand these nuances can build stronger relationships with international partners, tailor their solutions to meet local needs, and avoid potential misunderstandings. By appreciating and respecting cultural differences, innovators can create more inclusive and effective solutions.

Cultural nuances can have a significant impact on how products and services are perceived and received in different markets. Innovators who are attuned to these nuances can tailor their offerings to better meet the needs and preferences of diverse customer segments. This may involve adapting marketing strategies, product designs, or customer service approaches to align with local cultural norms and expectations. **By taking a culturally sensitive approach, innovators can create solutions that resonate more deeply with their target audiences.**

Understanding cultural nuances also requires effective communication skills. Innovators must be able to listen actively, ask thoughtful questions, and express themselves clearly and respectfully. This involves being open to feedback and willing to adapt one's approach based on the cultural context. **By developing strong communication skills, innovators can build trust and rapport with diverse stakeholders, fostering stronger and more productive relationships**.

Cultural insight goes beyond surface-level understanding—it requires a deep appreciation of the values and beliefs that shape different cultures. Innovators should take the time to learn about the history, traditions, and social dynamics of the markets they serve. This may involve conducting research, engaging with local communities, and seeking input from cultural experts. **By gaining a deeper understanding of cultural nuances, innovators can create solutions that are not only effective but also culturally respectful and relevant**.

6

Chapter 5: Understanding Cultural Nuances

In a globalized world, understanding cultural nuances is essential for innovators. Cultural insight involves recognizing the subtle differences in communication styles, values, and social norms across different cultures. Innovators who take the time to understand these nuances can build stronger relationships with international partners, tailor their solutions to meet local needs, and avoid potential misunderstandings. By appreciating and respecting cultural differences, innovators can create more inclusive and effective solutions.

Cultural nuances can have a significant impact on how products and services are perceived and received in different markets. Innovators who are attuned to these nuances can tailor their offerings to better meet the needs and preferences of diverse customer segments. This may involve adapting marketing strategies, product designs, or customer service approaches to align with local cultural norms and expectations. **By taking a culturally sensitive approach, innovators can create solutions that resonate more deeply with their target audiences.**

Understanding cultural nuances also requires effective communication skills. Innovators must be able to listen actively, ask thoughtful questions, and express themselves clearly and respectfully. This involves being open to feedback and willing to adapt one's approach based on the cultural context. **By developing strong communication skills, innovators can build trust and rapport with diverse stakeholders, fostering stronger and more productive relationships**.

Cultural insight goes beyond surface-level understanding—it requires a deep appreciation of the values and beliefs that shape different cultures. Innovators should take the time to learn about the history, traditions, and social dynamics of the markets they serve. This may involve conducting research, engaging with local communities, and seeking input from cultural experts. **By gaining a deeper understanding of cultural nuances, innovators can create solutions that are not only effective but also culturally respectful and relevant**.

Ultimately, understanding cultural nuances is about recognizing and valuing the unique contributions of each culture. Innovators who embrace cultural insight can create solutions that are more inclusive, equitable, and impactful. **By prioritizing cultural understanding, innovators can build stronger connections with their global audiences and create a lasting positive impact**.

7

Chapter 6: Ethical Decision-Making

Ethical decision-making is about making choices that are aligned with one's values and principles, even in the face of difficult dilemmas. Innovators often encounter situations where they must balance competing interests, such as profit versus social impact. Ethical decision-making involves considering the potential consequences of one's actions, seeking input from diverse stakeholders, and being willing to make sacrifices for the greater good. By prioritizing ethical considerations, innovators can build trust and credibility with their audience.

Ethical decision-making requires a strong foundation of integrity and transparency. Innovators must be honest in their communications, ensuring that stakeholders are fully informed about the potential impacts of their decisions. This involves being open to feedback and willing to engage in difficult conversations about the ethical implications of their actions. **By fostering a culture of transparency and accountability, innovators can create an environment where ethical decision-making is the norm.**

One of the key challenges of ethical decision-making is navigating the gray areas where the right course of action is not always clear. Innovators must be willing to grapple with complex ethical dilemmas, seeking input from diverse perspectives and weighing the potential consequences of their choices. This may involve consulting with ethics experts, engaging with stakeholders, and reflecting on one's own values and principles. **By taking a thoughtful**

and deliberate approach to ethical decision-making, innovators can navigate these challenges with integrity and confidence.

Ethical decision-making also involves a commitment to social responsibility. Innovators must consider the broader impact of their actions on society and the environment, striving to create solutions that benefit the greater good. This includes prioritizing sustainability, equity, and social justice in all aspects of their work. **By aligning their decisions with these principles, innovators can create a positive and lasting impact on the world**.

Ultimately, ethical decision-making is about doing what is right, even when it is difficult. Innovators who prioritize ethics in their decision-making processes can build trust and credibility with their stakeholders, creating a foundation for long-term success. **By leading with integrity and a commitment to ethical principles, innovators can create solutions that are not only effective but also responsible and sustainable**.

8

Chapter 7: Emotional Intelligence in Leadership

Effective leadership is rooted in emotional intelligence. Leaders who possess EI are able to inspire and motivate their teams, navigate conflicts with empathy, and create a positive work environment. They are skilled in recognizing and managing their own emotions, as well as understanding and influencing the emotions of others. By cultivating EI, leaders can foster a culture of innovation where team members feel valued, supported, and empowered to contribute their best ideas.

Emotional intelligence is essential for building strong and cohesive teams. Leaders who are attuned to the emotions of their team members can provide the support and encouragement needed to foster a positive and productive work environment. This involves recognizing and addressing the emotional needs of individuals, as well as creating opportunities for team members to connect and build relationships. **By prioritizing emotional intelligence, leaders can create a culture of trust and collaboration, where team members feel empowered to contribute their best work.**

Effective leaders also use emotional intelligence to navigate conflicts and challenges with empathy and grace. This involves listening actively, understanding different perspectives, and finding solutions that address the underlying emotional needs of all parties involved. **By approaching con-**

flicts with empathy, leaders can create a more harmonious and resilient work environment, where challenges are viewed as opportunities for growth and learning.

Emotional intelligence is also crucial for inspiring and motivating teams. Leaders who possess EI can connect with their team members on a deeper level, understanding their passions and motivations, and aligning them with the goals of the organization. This involves recognizing and celebrating the unique contributions of each team member, providing regular feedback and encouragement, and creating opportunities for growth and development. **By fostering a culture of emotional intelligence, leaders can create a motivated and engaged workforce, driving innovation and success**.

Ultimately, emotional intelligence is about creating a positive and supportive work environment where team members feel valued and empowered. Leaders who cultivate EI can build strong and cohesive teams, navigate challenges with empathy and grace, and inspire their teams to achieve their best work. **By prioritizing emotional intelligence in leadership, innovators can create a culture of innovation and excellence, driving their organizations forward.**

9

Chapter 8: Cultural Adaptability

Cultural adaptability is the ability to navigate and thrive in diverse cultural settings. For innovators, this quality is essential as they seek to expand their reach into new markets. Cultural adaptability involves being open-minded, flexible, and willing to learn from different cultural perspectives. Innovators who are culturally adaptable can build stronger relationships with diverse stakeholders, tailor their solutions to meet local needs, and create more inclusive and impactful innovations.

Cultural adaptability requires a willingness to step outside of one's comfort zone and embrace new experiences. Innovators must be open to learning from different cultures, recognizing the value of diverse perspectives, and being willing to adapt their approaches based on the cultural context. This involves being curious, asking questions, and seeking out opportunities to engage with different cultural communities. **By fostering a mindset of openness and curiosity, innovators can develop the cultural adaptability needed to thrive in a globalized world**.

Effective communication is also key to cultural adaptability. Innovators must be able to communicate clearly and respectfully across cultural boundaries, recognizing and addressing potential misunderstandings. This involves being mindful of cultural norms and communication styles, and adapting one's approach based on the needs and preferences of different stakeholders. **By developing strong communication skills, innovators can build trust** and rapport with diverse stakeholders, fostering stronger and more productive relationships**.

Cultural adaptability also involves being flexible and willing to change one's approach based on the cultural context. Innovators must be able to recognize when their existing strategies and solutions are not effective in a particular cultural setting, and be willing to adapt and iterate based on feedback. This may involve making changes to product designs, marketing strategies, or business models to better align with local needs and preferences. **By being flexible and adaptable, innovators can create solutions that are more relevant and impactful in different cultural contexts**.

Ultimately, cultural adaptability is about recognizing and valuing the unique contributions of different cultures, and being willing to learn and grow from diverse perspectives. Innovators who prioritize cultural adaptability can create more inclusive and effective solutions, building stronger connections with their global audiences. **By embracing cultural adaptability, innovators can create a positive and lasting impact on the world, fostering a more inclusive and interconnected global community**.

10

Chapter 8: Cultural Adaptability

Cultural adaptability is the ability to navigate and thrive in diverse cultural settings. For innovators, this quality is essential as they seek to expand their reach into new markets. Cultural adaptability involves being open-minded, flexible, and willing to learn from different cultural perspectives. Innovators who are culturally adaptable can build stronger relationships with diverse stakeholders, tailor their solutions to meet local needs, and create more inclusive and impactful innovations.

Cultural adaptability requires a willingness to step outside of one's comfort zone and embrace new experiences. Innovators must be open to learning from different cultures, recognizing the value of diverse perspectives, and being willing to adapt their approaches based on the cultural context. This involves being curious, asking questions, and seeking out opportunities to engage with different cultural communities. **By fostering a mindset of openness and curiosity, innovators can develop the cultural adaptability needed to thrive in a globalized world**.

Effective communication is also key to cultural adaptability. Innovators must be able to communicate clearly and respectfully across cultural boundaries, recognizing and addressing potential misunderstandings. This involves being mindful of cultural norms and communication styles, and adapting one's approach based on the needs and preferences of different stakeholders. **By developing strong communication skills, innovators can build trust** and rapport with diverse stakeholders, fostering stronger and more productive relationships**.

Cultural adaptability also involves being flexible and willing to change one's approach based on the cultural context. Innovators must be able to recognize when their existing strategies and solutions are not effective in a particular cultural setting, and be willing to adapt and iterate based on feedback. This may involve making changes to product designs, marketing strategies, or business models to better align with local needs and preferences. **By being flexible and adaptable, innovators can create solutions that are more relevant and impactful in different cultural contexts**.

Ultimately, cultural adaptability is about recognizing and valuing the unique contributions of different cultures, and being willing to learn and grow from diverse perspectives. Innovators who prioritize cultural adaptability can create more inclusive and effective solutions, building stronger connections with their global audiences. **By embracing cultural adaptability, innovators can create a positive and lasting impact on the world, fostering a more inclusive and interconnected global community**.

11

Chapter 9: Ethical Entrepreneurship in Practice

Ethical entrepreneurship is not just a theoretical concept—it's a practical approach to doing business. Innovators can incorporate ethical principles into their daily operations by setting clear ethical standards, creating a code of conduct, and ensuring accountability through regular audits and feedback mechanisms. By embedding ethics into the fabric of their organizations, innovators can create a culture of integrity and trust that supports long-term success.

Setting clear ethical standards is the first step in practicing ethical entrepreneurship. Innovators should define their core values and principles, and communicate these standards to all stakeholders. This involves creating a code of conduct that outlines expected behaviors and provides guidance on how to handle ethical dilemmas. **By establishing a strong ethical foundation, innovators can create a framework for decision-making that prioritizes integrity and responsibility.**

Regular audits and feedback mechanisms are essential for ensuring accountability and transparency. Innovators should conduct regular reviews of their operations, assessing compliance with ethical standards and identifying areas for improvement. This may involve engaging with external auditors, seeking input from stakeholders, and implementing corrective actions as needed.

By maintaining a culture of accountability, innovators can build trust with their stakeholders and ensure that ethical principles are upheld in all aspects of their work.

Ethical entrepreneurship also involves a commitment to continuous improvement. Innovators should regularly evaluate their practices and seek opportunities to enhance their ethical standards. This may involve staying informed about emerging ethical issues, engaging with industry experts, and participating in professional development opportunities. **By prioritizing continuous improvement, innovators can stay ahead of ethical challenges and create a more sustainable and responsible business.**

Ultimately, ethical entrepreneurship is about creating a culture of integrity and responsibility that supports long-term success. Innovators who prioritize ethical principles in their daily operations can build trust and credibility with their stakeholders, creating a foundation for lasting impact. **By embedding ethics into the fabric of their organizations, innovators can create a positive and enduring legacy, inspiring others to follow in their footsteps and make a difference in the world.**

12

Chapter 10: Emotional Intelligence in Collaboration

Collaboration is a key driver of innovation, and emotional intelligence plays a crucial role in effective collaboration. Innovators who possess EI are able to build strong, cohesive teams, navigate conflicts with empathy, and create a positive and productive working environment. They are skilled in recognizing and managing their own emotions, as well as understanding and influencing the emotions of others. By cultivating EI, innovators can foster a culture of collaboration where team members feel valued, supported, and empowered to contribute their best ideas.

Emotional intelligence is essential for building trust and rapport within teams. Innovators who are attuned to the emotions of their team members can provide the support and encouragement needed to foster a positive and collaborative work environment. This involves recognizing and addressing the emotional needs of individuals, as well as creating opportunities for team members to connect and build relationships. **By prioritizing emotional intelligence, innovators can create a culture of trust and collaboration, where team members feel empowered to contribute their best work**.

Effective collaboration also requires navigating conflicts with empathy and grace. Innovators who possess EI can approach conflicts with a focus on understanding different perspectives and finding solutions that address the underlying emotional needs of all parties involved. This involves listening actively, expressing empathy, and seeking common ground. **By approaching conflicts with empathy, innovators can create a more harmonious and resilient work environment, where challenges are viewed as opportunities for growth and learning.**

Emotional intelligence is also crucial for fostering creativity and innovation within teams. Innovators who possess EI can create an environment where team members feel safe to share their ideas and take risks. This involves recognizing and celebrating the unique contributions of each team member, providing regular feedback and encouragement, and creating opportunities for growth and development. **By fostering a culture of emotional intelligence, innovators can create a motivated and engaged workforce, driving innovation and success.**

Ultimately, emotional intelligence is about creating a positive and supportive work environment where team members feel valued and empowered. Innovators who cultivate EI can build strong and cohesive teams, navigate conflicts with empathy and grace, and inspire their teams to achieve their best work. **By prioritizing emotional intelligence in collaboration, innovators can create a culture of innovation and excellence, driving their organizations forward.**

13

Chapter 11: Cultural Insight in Market Research

Market research is a critical component of the innovation process, and cultural insight is essential for understanding the needs and preferences of different customer segments. Innovators who take the time to conduct thorough market research can uncover hidden opportunities, tailor their solutions to meet local needs, and create more effective marketing strategies. By leveraging cultural insight in market research, innovators can create products and services that resonate with diverse audiences.

Effective market research requires a deep understanding of the cultural context of different markets. Innovators must be able to recognize and appreciate the unique values, beliefs, and behaviors that shape consumer preferences in different cultural settings. This involves conducting qualitative and quantitative research, engaging with local communities, and seeking input from cultural experts. **By gaining a deeper understanding of cultural nuances, innovators can create solutions that are more relevant and impactful.**

Cultural insight is also crucial for identifying and addressing potential barriers to adoption. Innovators must be able to recognize and address cultural factors that may influence how products and services are perceived and received. This may involve adapting marketing messages, product designs, or customer service approaches to align with local cultural norms and expectations. **By taking a culturally sensitive approach, innovators can create solutions that resonate more deeply with their target audiences.**

Market research should also involve continuous learning and adaptation. Innovators should regularly evaluate their market research efforts and seek opportunities to enhance their understanding of different cultural contexts. This may involve staying informed about emerging cultural trends, engaging with industry experts, and participating in professional development opportunities. **By prioritizing continuous learning, innovators can stay ahead of cultural changes and create more effective and sustainable solutions.**

Ultimately, cultural insight is about recognizing and valuing the unique contributions of different cultures, and being willing to learn and grow from diverse perspectives. Innovators who prioritize cultural insight in their market research can create more inclusive and effective solutions, building stronger connections with their global audiences. **By leveraging cultural insight in market research, innovators can create a positive and lasting impact on the world, fostering a more inclusive and interconnected global community.**

14

Chapter 12: Ethical Marketing

Ethical marketing is about promoting products and services in a way that is honest, transparent, and respectful of consumers. Innovators must be mindful of the impact of their marketing strategies on different customer segments, and avoid tactics that are deceptive, manipulative, or discriminatory. Ethical marketing involves being transparent about the features and benefits of products, respecting customer privacy, and prioritizing long-term relationships over short-term gains. By adopting ethical marketing practices, innovators can build trust and credibility with their audience.

Transparency is a cornerstone of ethical marketing. Innovators must ensure that their marketing messages accurately represent their products and services, without exaggeration or deception. This involves providing clear and honest information about product features, benefits, and potential limitations. **By being transparent in their marketing efforts, innovators can build trust with their consumers and foster long-term loyalty**.

Respecting customer privacy is another key aspect of ethical marketing. Innovators must be mindful of how they collect, use, and store customer data, ensuring that they comply with privacy regulations and respect consumer preferences. This involves being transparent about data collection practices, providing clear opt-in and opt-out options, and safeguarding customer information from unauthorized access. **By prioritizing customer privacy,**

innovators can build a reputation for integrity and trustworthiness.

Ethical marketing also involves a commitment to social responsibility. Innovators should consider the broader impact of their marketing strategies on society and the environment, avoiding tactics that perpetuate harmful stereotypes or contribute to environmental degradation. This may involve promoting products that are environmentally friendly, supporting social causes, or engaging in fair trade practices. **By aligning their marketing efforts with their ethical principles, innovators can create a positive impact and differentiate themselves in the marketplace**.

Ultimately, ethical marketing is about creating value for consumers while maintaining a commitment to integrity and responsibility. Innovators who prioritize ethical marketing practices can build trust and credibility with their audience, fostering long-term relationships and driving sustainable success. **By adopting ethical marketing principles, innovators can create a positive and lasting impact on their customers and the world**.

15

Chapter 13: Emotional Intelligence in Negotiation

Negotiation is a critical skill for innovators, and emotional intelligence plays a crucial role in successful negotiation. Innovators who possess EI are able to navigate complex negotiations with empathy, build strong relationships with negotiating partners, and achieve mutually beneficial outcomes. They are skilled in recognizing and managing their own emotions, as well as understanding and influencing the emotions of others. By cultivating EI, innovators can become more effective negotiators and achieve better outcomes in their business dealings.

Emotional intelligence is essential for building rapport and trust in negotiations. Innovators who are attuned to the emotions of their negotiating partners can create a positive and collaborative atmosphere, fostering open communication and mutual respect. This involves recognizing and addressing the emotional needs of both parties, as well as demonstrating empathy and understanding. **By prioritizing emotional intelligence, innovators can build stronger relationships with their negotiating partners and achieve more successful outcomes**.

Effective negotiators also use emotional intelligence to navigate conflicts and challenges with grace and empathy. This involves listening actively, understanding different perspectives, and finding solutions that address the underlying emotional needs of all parties involved. **By approaching conflicts with empathy, negotiators can create a more harmonious and productive negotiation process, leading to better outcomes for all parties.**

Emotional intelligence is also crucial for managing one's own emotions during negotiations. Innovators must be able to remain calm and composed, even in high-pressure situations, and avoid letting emotions cloud their judgment. This involves developing self-awareness, recognizing one's own emotional triggers, and employing strategies to manage stress and maintain focus. **By cultivating emotional intelligence, negotiators can maintain a clear and objective perspective, making more informed and effective decisions.**

Ultimately, emotional intelligence is about creating a positive and collaborative negotiation process that leads to mutually beneficial outcomes. Innovators who possess EI can build stronger relationships with their negotiating partners, navigate conflicts with empathy, and achieve better outcomes in their business dealings. **By prioritizing emotional intelligence in negotiation, innovators can create a more successful and sustainable approach to business.**

16

Chapter 14: Cultural Sensitivity in Product Development

Cultural sensitivity is essential for developing products and services that meet the needs of diverse customer segments. Innovators who take the time to understand the cultural context of their target markets can create solutions that are more relevant and impactful. Cultural sensitivity involves being mindful of cultural norms, values, and preferences, and incorporating these insights into the design and development process. By prioritizing cultural sensitivity in product development, innovators can create more inclusive and effective solutions.

Cultural sensitivity requires a deep understanding of the cultural context of different markets. Innovators must be able to recognize and appreciate the unique values, beliefs, and behaviors that shape consumer preferences in different cultural settings. This involves conducting qualitative and quantitative research, engaging with local communities, and seeking input from cultural experts. **By gaining a deeper understanding of cultural nuances, innovators can create solutions that are more relevant and impactful.**

Effective product development also involves incorporating cultural insights into the design and development process. Innovators should consider how cultural factors may influence the usability and appeal of their products, and make design decisions that align with local cultural norms and preferences. This may involve adapting product features, packaging, or marketing strategies to better resonate with different cultural segments. **By taking a culturally sensitive approach, innovators can create products that are more inclusive and effective in different cultural contexts.**

Cultural sensitivity also requires ongoing learning and adaptation. Innovators should regularly evaluate their product development efforts and seek opportunities to enhance their understanding of different cultural contexts. This may involve staying informed about emerging cultural trends, engaging with industry experts, and participating in professional development opportunities. **By prioritizing continuous learning, innovators can stay ahead of cultural changes and create more effective and sustainable solutions.**

Ultimately, cultural sensitivity is about recognizing and valuing the unique contributions of different cultures, and being willing to learn and grow from diverse perspectives. Innovators who prioritize cultural sensitivity in product development can create more inclusive and effective solutions, building stronger connections with their global audiences. **By embracing cultural sensitivity, innovators can create a positive and lasting impact on the world, fostering a more inclusive and interconnected global community.**

17

Chapter 15: Ethical Supply Chain Management

Ethical supply chain management is about ensuring that the entire supply chain operates in a way that is aligned with ethical principles. Innovators must be mindful of the impact of their supply chain decisions on workers, communities, and the environment. Ethical supply chain management involves setting clear ethical standards, conducting regular audits, and collaborating with suppliers to address any issues that arise. By prioritizing ethical supply chain management, innovators can create a more sustainable and responsible business.

Setting clear ethical standards is the first step in ethical supply chain management. Innovators should define their core values and principles, and communicate these standards to all stakeholders in the supply chain. This involves creating a code of conduct that outlines expected behaviors and provides guidance on how to handle ethical dilemmas. **By establishing a strong ethical foundation, innovators can create a framework for decision-making that prioritizes integrity and responsibility**.

Regular audits and feedback mechanisms are essential for ensuring accountability and transparency in the supply chain. Innovators should conduct regular reviews of their supply chain operations, assessing compliance with ethical standards and identifying areas for improvement. This may involve engaging with external auditors, seeking input from stakeholders, and implementing corrective actions as needed. **By maintaining a culture of accountability, innovators can build trust with their stakeholders and ensure that ethical principles are upheld in all aspects of their work.**

Ethical supply chain management also involves collaboration with suppliers to address any issues that arise. Innovators should work closely with their suppliers to identify and resolve ethical challenges, providing support and resources as needed. This may involve developing training programs, conducting regular audits, and implementing corrective actions to address any issues. **By collaborating with suppliers, innovators can create a more responsible and sustainable supply chain, fostering positive relationships and driving long-term success.**

Ultimately, ethical supply chain management is about creating a culture of integrity and responsibility that supports long-term success. Innovators who prioritize ethical principles in their supply chain operations can build trust and credibility with their stakeholders, creating a foundation for lasting impact. **By embedding ethics into the fabric of their supply chain, innovators can create a positive and enduring legacy, inspiring others to follow in their footsteps and make a difference in the world.**

Chapter 16: Emotional Intelligence in Customer Relations Customer relations are a critical component of business success, and emotional intelligence plays a crucial role in building strong relationships with customers. Innovators who possess EI are able to understand and empathize with customer needs, address concerns with empathy, and create positive and lasting relationships. They are skilled in recognizing and managing their own emotions, as well as understanding and influencing the emotions of customers. By cultivating EI in customer relations, innovators can create a loyal and satisfied customer base.

Emotional intelligence is essential for understanding and empathizing with customer needs. Innovators who are attuned to the emotions of their customers can provide the support and encouragement needed to foster positive and lasting relationships. This involves recognizing and addressing the emotional needs of customers, as well as creating opportunities for meaningful interactions. **By prioritizing emotional intelligence, innovators can create a culture of trust and collaboration, where customers feel valued and supported.**

Effective customer relations also require navigating conflicts and challenges with empathy and grace. Innovators who possess EI can approach customer concerns with a focus on understanding different perspectives and finding solutions that address the underlying emotional needs of all parties involved. This involves listening actively, expressing empathy, and seeking common ground. **By approaching conflicts with empathy, innovators can create a more harmonious and productive customer relationship process, leading to better outcomes for all parties.**

Emotional intelligence is also crucial for inspiring and motivating customers. Innovators who possess EI can connect with their customers on a deeper level, understanding their passions and motivations, and aligning them with the goals

18

Chapter 16: Emotional Intelligence in Customer Relations

Customer relations are a critical component of business success, and emotional intelligence plays a crucial role in building strong relationships with customers. Innovators who possess EI are able to understand and empathize with customer needs, address concerns with empathy, and create positive and lasting relationships. They are skilled in recognizing and managing their own emotions, as well as understanding and influencing the emotions of customers. By cultivating EI in customer relations, innovators can create a loyal and satisfied customer base.

Emotional intelligence is essential for understanding and empathizing with customer needs. Innovators who are attuned to the emotions of their customers can provide the support and encouragement needed to foster positive and lasting relationships. This involves recognizing and addressing the emotional needs of customers, as well as creating opportunities for meaningful interactions. **By prioritizing emotional intelligence, innovators can create a culture of trust and collaboration, where customers feel valued and supported**.

Effective customer relations also require navigating conflicts and challenges with empathy and grace. Innovators who possess EI can approach customer concerns with a focus on understanding different perspectives and finding

CHAPTER 16: EMOTIONAL INTELLIGENCE IN CUSTOMER RELATIONS

solutions that address the underlying emotional needs of all parties involved. This involves listening actively, expressing empathy, and seeking common ground. **By approaching conflicts with empathy, innovators can create a more harmonious and productive customer relationship process, leading to better outcomes for all parties.**

Emotional intelligence is also crucial for inspiring and motivating customers. Innovators who possess EI can connect with their customers on a deeper level, understanding their passions and motivations, and aligning them with the goals of the organization. This involves recognizing and celebrating the unique contributions of each customer, providing regular feedback and encouragement, and creating opportunities for growth and development. **By fostering a culture of emotional intelligence, innovators can create a loyal and satisfied customer base, driving long-term success.**

Ultimately, emotional intelligence in customer relations is about creating a positive and supportive experience for customers, where they feel valued and understood. Innovators who cultivate EI can build strong and lasting relationships with their customers, navigate challenges with empathy and grace, and inspire loyalty and satisfaction. **By prioritizing emotional intelligence in customer relations, innovators can create a positive and lasting impact on their customers and the world.**

19

Chapter 17: The Future of Ethical Innovation

The future of innovation lies in the intersection of emotional intelligence, cultural insight, and ethical entrepreneurship. As the world becomes more interconnected and complex, the ability to navigate these dimensions will become increasingly important for innovators. By prioritizing emotional intelligence, cultural insight, and ethical principles, innovators can create solutions that are not only innovative but also meaningful, inclusive, and sustainable. The future belongs to those who lead with their hearts and minds, and who are committed to making a positive impact on the world.

The evolving landscape of innovation requires a deep commitment to emotional intelligence. Innovators who can navigate the complexities of human emotions and relationships will be better positioned to create solutions that resonate on a deeper level with their audience. This involves developing self-awareness, empathy, and effective communication skills, and fostering a culture of emotional intelligence within their organizations. **By prioritizing emotional intelligence, innovators can create a more compassionate and inclusive approach to innovation, driving meaningful social change.**

Cultural insight will also play a crucial role in the future of innovation.

Innovators who can understand and appreciate the unique contributions of different cultures will be better positioned to create solutions that are relevant and impactful. This involves conducting thorough market research, engaging with local communities, and seeking input from cultural experts. **By prioritizing cultural insight, innovators can create more inclusive and effective solutions, building stronger connections with their global audiences**.

Ethical entrepreneurship will be the cornerstone of sustainable innovation. Innovators who are guided by a strong sense of integrity and responsibility will be better positioned to create solutions that benefit the greater good. This involves setting clear ethical standards, conducting regular audits, and collaborating with stakeholders to address any issues. **By prioritizing ethical principles, innovators can create a positive and lasting impact on the world, fostering a culture of integrity and trust**.

Ultimately, the future of innovation belongs to those who can navigate the intersection of emotional intelligence, cultural insight, and ethical entrepreneurship. Innovators who prioritize these dimensions can create solutions that are not only innovative but also meaningful, inclusive, and sustainable. **By leading with their hearts and minds, innovators can create a positive and enduring legacy, inspiring others to follow in their footsteps and make a difference in the world**.

Book Description:

In "The Innovator's Heart: Emotional Intelligence, Cultural Insight, and Ethical Entrepreneurship," readers are invited on a transformative journey through the core principles that drive meaningful and sustainable innovation. This book delves into the intersection of emotional intelligence, cultural insight, and ethical entrepreneurship, offering a comprehensive guide for innovators seeking to make a positive impact on the world.

Through seventeen engaging chapters, the book explores the importance of emotional intelligence in fostering strong, cohesive teams and creating solutions that resonate on a deeper level with audiences. It highlights the value of cultural diversity and sensitivity, showing how understanding different perspectives can lead to groundbreaking ideas and inclusive innovations.

The book also emphasizes the significance of ethical decision-making and responsible entrepreneurship, providing practical strategies for building a culture of integrity and trust.

Filled with practical insights, real-world examples, and actionable strategies, "The Innovator's Heart" is an essential read for anyone looking to navigate the complexities of the modern innovation landscape. Whether you're an aspiring entrepreneur, a seasoned business leader, or simply someone passionate about making a difference, this book offers the tools and inspiration you need to lead with your heart and mind.

www.ingramcontent.com/pod-product-compliance
Lightning Source LLC
LaVergne TN
LVHW020455080526
838202LV00057B/5968